HEARTBEATS OF HINDUISM

LIVING THE TRUTH
OF THE IMMORTAL DHARMA

DAVID SAMNGA-LASTRI

HEARTBEATS
OF
HINDUISM

*Living the Truth of
the Immortal Dharma*

SOPHIA PERENNIS

SAN RAFAEL, CA

For information, address:
Sophia Perennis, P.O. Box 151011
San Rafael, CA 94915
sophiaperennis.com

Library of Congress Cataloging-in-Publication Data

Samnga-Lastri, David.
Heartbeats of Hinduism : living the truth of the immortal dharma
/ David Samnga-Lastri.—1st ed.

p. cm.
ISBN 1 59731 062 X (pbk: alk. paper)
ISBN 1 59731 063 8 (hardcover: alk. paper)
1. Hindu meditations. 2. Krishna (Hindu deity)
—Prayer-books and devotions—English. I. Title
BL1236.22.S255   2006
294.5'432—dc22   2006021557

*Dedicated to
Huston Smith,*

Our Teacher and Friend

INTRODUCTION

MUCH OF THE explanatory, occasionally inferential material in this Introduction to *Heartbeats of Hinduism* is based upon my own reading of it informed by my background as a Vedantist. The remainder, dealing with its origins and method of composition, emerges from my email communications with the author, David Samnga-Lastri, and from one rather brief personal interview.

We have here a collection of what the author called 'affirmations'. I am satisfied that they could only have emerged from direct experience, and this also is the author's claim. What is this 'direct experience'? The term is widely employed in the Eastern traditions and refers to an unmediated experience of the divine reality, a vision of that reality in which the world and the meditator are transfigured, revealed for what they truly are and were all along, attained, or 'received', as a gift of grace, in that higher state of consciousness, in the Hindu tradition called *turiya*, or 'the fourth state', which is the goal of meditation. The quality of direct experience is a bliss, peace and love perceived without doubt as infinite and eternal and as the very essence of our humanity and the universe, and an ecstatic certitude of being in the presence of, and one with, absolute truth or reality: God. The permutations of this experience are inexhaustible, as the recorded words of the great sages implicitly testify and explicitly proclaim. And the experience—a very important point—occurs in its fullness only within the framework of a revealed doctrine, a spiritual tradition. In the present case, the religion of India, Hinduism.

The affirmations in this book 'came to' Samnga-Lastri roughly between December 2004 and December 2005; he had been a practitioner of Hinduism for over thirty years. At first he wrote them down without thinking of them as the content of a book, but to preserve them for future reference as a means of awakening and recovering the experience they described and from which they emerged. In time, of course, it became clear to him that they could serve an analogous function for others. This book is being published in the hope that it may facilitate that goal.

There are many, actually countless, Hindu *dharmas*, or versions of practice and interpretation. Samnga-Lastri's practice and experience seem to combine the *bhagavata dharma—bhakti*, the Path of Love, worship and adoration of the Personal God, the avatar, culminating in Union through Love—and the *adhyatma yoga, jnana*, the Path of Knowledge, culminating in identity with the Impersonal Absolute or *Brahman* through the Path of discrimination between the Real and the Unreal, between the illusory 'lower self' or ego and the true Self or *Atman: Brahman* and *Atman* are One—although it could be argued, and has been, persuasively, that each one includes the other. (An explication of these two Paths can be found in the Introduction to my *Eastern Light in Western Eyes*, also published by Sophia Perennis.) The avatar in Samnga-Lastri's practice is Krishna, sometimes called 'the Christ of India'. His teaching and captivating, for many people convincing spiritual 'presence' are found in the *Bhagavad Gita* and the *Srimad Bhagavatam*. For the former I recommend the fine translation by Swami Prabhavananda and Christopher Isherwood, for the latter the excellent abridged version also translated by Prabhavananda. One of the achievements, I believe, actually the principal achievement, of Samnga-Lastri's text is that he has somehow managed to circumvent or bypass the metaphysical intricacies of the 'personal/impersonal' discussion in Hinduism by translating them into, again, statements of direct experience, in a language, a poetic idiom, combining extreme simplicity with adequate depth. The challenge to the reader is not to understand the words, which is easy enough, but to enter into the experience they articulate, which requires an intuition of their truth and the serious determination to realize it in one's own life. That this challenge offers an opportunity on the highest level goes without saying.

Samnga-Lastri's text, on the surface, is sufficiently transparent to be read without explanation, but references might be helpful.

SOME VOCABULARY. THERE ARE A FEW SANSKRIT TERMS

Param Purusam, Purushottama: the Personal God, Supreme Person.

So'ham: I am That, meaning, I am *Brahman*, the *Atman*, the Self of the Universe, the I-Consciousness of the Universe, the Self-Awareness of the Universe which *is* the Universe.

Maya: the world-appearance, the phenomenal world, the 'here below', the Manifestation, the Great Dream.

Santim Nirvana Paramam: the Supreme Peace of Nirvana.

OM Namah Krishnaya: Homage, Salutations, to Lord Krishna.

ENGLISH LANGUAGE USAGES

'All this'. Everything, the whole world, everything we know and see.

'I AM': A Name of God.

'The One I AM': In his very frequent use of this term (and similar constructions, such as 'The Light, that I AM, is God', 'Thou art the One I AM', 'The Self, that I AM, is Peace') Samnga-Lastri is quite probably exploiting the fact that in the English language the word 'that', either expressed or implied, is both a reflexive and a demonstrative pronoun. Thus, for example, the phrase, 'The One I AM' can mean both 'myself', the speaker, and/or God, the worshipper and/or Krishna, a double meaning exactly consistent with the Truth proclaimed by the doctrine, the identity of *Atman* and *Brahman*. Even the single word 'I' often implies, so it seems, this double meaning.

'The Self': Directly from most translations of the *Upanishads*: the *Atman*.

'The Name', 'Thy Name': The Name of God is a mantra, and it is often held that God is present in His Name, in the worshipful enunciation of the Holy Name. This mantra function of the Name of God, in the present text Krishna, clearly has special significance for Samnga-Lastri. Invocation of the Name is discussed in *Eastern Light in Western Eyes*.

The author, in most of the affirmations, makes a subtle use of rhyme, usually in the closing lines. As he explained to me, line length, line breaks and rhythm, poetic effects, were also on his mind as he sought to frame the fragments of text which came to him in meditation, although at times the entire text was transcribed without change. Editing was impossible without re-immersing himself in the meditative vision or insight.

How might this text be read? To whom is it addressed? As far as the second question goes, it was originally addressed to Samnga-Lastri himself. By extension it is addressed to those who are interested in the religion of India and wish some entry into its comprehension. The religion of India has inspired countless 'introductory' texts, many of them quite excellent. What distinguishes this volume is its unwavering focus upon, again, direct experience rather than historical survey or elucidation of doctrine. The *Bhagavad Gita, Upanishads, Brahma Sutras, Viveka Chudamani, Panchadasi, Yoga Vasishtha, Ashtavakra Samhita, Narada Bhakti Sutras, Srimad Bhagavatam, Siva Sutras, Ramayana*, etc., as well as the many inspired commentaries, familiarity with which is implied, are never even mentioned; they or their messages, we are invited to suppose, have been assimilated and internalized by the author and now inform the crystallized articulation of his ecstatic experience. The goal of the reader is to enter into the state of mind or soul from which the affirmations emerge. That the text is thematically repetitive, or insistent, is only to be expected: so are the holy *Upanishads* and the writing of the mystics in all spiritual traditions. Given its infinite importance, its life-and-death nature, its inherent opposition to the distractions and insidious seductions of worldliness, especially pervasive in these times, the spiritual Truth, it appears and with good reason, demands to be hammered home from every direction available. We are urged toward the 'perpetual remembrance of God'.

Depending upon individual inclination, the text, it seems to me, might be read straight through, aiming at an overall effect, something gradually 'sinking in'; or the reader may concentrate upon one affirmation at a time, pronounce it slowly, try to experience it as his or her own words, his or her own voice speaking: seek direct experience. The *Bhagavad Gita*, usually regarded as the single most representative text in the Hindu tradition, would certainly be an excellent companion volume.

While Buddhist groups are everywhere present in this society, I regret to say that Hinduism cannot make a similar claim: far to the contrary. There are scattered groups, nearly all of them cults of a particular 'god-man', living or dead, which the reader may approach, with the appropriate caution, for companionship and support.

The four-word last line of one of Samnga-Lastri's affirmations is a direct quote from Shakespeare—*Hamlet*, I believe. See if you can find it!

MARTY GLASS

*The Vedanta can be known
only to the extent that it has been lived.*

— A. K. Coomaraswamy —

In Thy Silence is the Universe.
This is Reality:
Thy Silent Presence,
Here in the candle-light.
Heart of the Universe,
Heart of my Heart,
I live only to return to Thy Presence,
Disappear into Thy Presence
And never leave again.
When, O my Beloved, when?
When?

The Dream vanishes into the Dreamer—
The Dreamer alone remains.
The sun still shines,
The birds fly overhead,
The trees sway in the breeze,
It's clear or it rains.
But in my Heart I kneel:
The Dreamer alone is Real.

The thought that Thou art,
That Thou art the Self,
The Self of the Universe,
My very Self, the One I AM,
Floods my Heart with Joy,
The Joy that Thou art.
The thought that Thou art
Is the Joy that Thou art
O Beloved Lord,
O Krishna.

Another morning
In the Eternal Now.
It is Krishna,
The Eternal Thou.
Time came, Time went,
Time is gone:
Eternal Krishna,
Eternal Dawn.
Thou alone,
The world is gone,
Eternal Peace,
Eternal Beloved,
The Peace of God,
My Eternal Heart:
This Eternal Dawn.

OM So'ham
With every breath.
No thoughts of this world.
The Truth…
Or endless birth-and-death.

This is the miracle:
That Thou art enshrined
In Thy Name. In Thy Name
I seek Thee, and by Thy Grace
I find Thee, in Thy Name:
In Thy Name in my mind,
And Thee in Thy Name.
Thy Name is my Treasure,
Thy Name is the Universe,
The whole world sings Thy Name.
I am wined and dined
In the Bliss of Thy Name.
Blessed be Thy Holy Name,
The Holy Name of God.
Krishna.

There is only Now,
There is only Thou.
Thou, Now, Forever.
That's it. That's all.

Love is the Answer:
It never fails.
Love someone, put a smile
On someone's face:
Love prevails.
Love rescues and heals,
Blooms, endures, prevails.
But the Love of God
Wakes us from this Dream
And fills the Universe.
I live only for that Love,
That Infinite Love,
That Love Supreme.

Whatever it is,
Nothing will come of it.
Forget it,
Stop thinking about it.
It's nothing
And nothing will come of it.
Everything is Nothing.
Know this as Joy,
Peace, Freedom.
Salvation.
Remember Krishna.
The Beloved.

Thou art all of us,
Every life, every story.
O Great Dreamer of Worlds,
Who can sing thy Glory?
Thou the Dreamer, Thou the Dream.
Lord of Light. Joy Supreme.

There's Light,
There's a World,
And they are One,
Called the Self:
The One I AM.
That's all there is,
No room for anything else.
Then who am I?
I who meditate, and smile,
And know I will never die?
Who am I, O Krishna?
O Krishna of my Heart?
Who am I?

If it happens, it's not real:
What's real simply IS—
Changeless, eternal, forever.
Our lives, as we live them,
Are nothing. The world is His.
The world is He, the world is His.

Lord of Night,
Lord of Day,
The One, the All,
The Truth, the Way.
In Thee we live.
To Thee we pray.

Who am I?
Eternal Bliss.
What am I?
The world: all this.

Earth and Sky,
Stars and Sun,
Thou art the All,
The Self, the One.

Don't want anything.
Just move through the day
Taking care of things
As they arise. Realize:
Here is no place,
Now is no time,
There is nothing,
I am no one.
God alone is Real.
Recall this Truth,
The wisdom of the wise,
At the close of the day,
In the silence and repose
When you meditate and pray,
And nothing remains
But the Self Who never dies.

I can see
Ahead of me
Extinction in Thee.
No world,
No me,
Nothing but Thee.
Peace.

Lord of Day,
Lord of light,
Lord of Love,
Lord of Light.

There are all
These things of the world,
Items on my lists.
They are nothing.
The world is nothing.
God alone exists.

No past, no future:
Just the Eternal Now.
No world, nothing:
Just the Eternal Thou.

There's nothing I need to hear,
Nothing I wish to say.
I am no longer here.
I have gone away.
I will return,
In the role I play,
But I'll only stay
As long as I need to stay.
There's nothing here.
And one day I'll go away
Never to return again.
I don't know when.
It's not up to me.
I'm one who waits and prays.
There won't be a call:
One of these days
I'll just suddenly know.
The readiness is all.

This is the Self.
The One I AM.
Here and Now.
Buddha-Nature.
The Lord of Love.
Allah. The Tao.

In beautiful things,
I am the beauty.
In fair weather,
I am the fairness.
In silent bliss,
I am the silence.
I am the Self of all.
I am Awareness.

There is nothing,
There is no one.
No need to give a damn.
There's only remembering
Or forgetting God:
The One I AM.

In pure hearts,
I am the purity.
In serene spirits,
I am the serenity.
In tranquil acceptance,
I am the tranquillity.
In humble submission,
I am the humility.
I am Eternity,
And I am Infinity.
I alone am Reality.
I am Krishna.

Everything I have
Ever known was God.
Everything I remember
Doing, hearing, seeing.
Everything in the here
And now: also God.
His Infinite Life,
Infinite Joy: His Being.

I am Thee,
Thou art me:
We are One.
One are We.
I am Thine,
Thou art mine:
My very Heart,
O Light Divine.

I'm already gone,
Already the Universe,
Already the past, present and future,
Already everything that's happened,
Is happening or will happen,
Everything that was, is or will be,
Already the Infinite Consciousness,
The Self, the Light,
Already Absence and Presence,
The empty space
Where a world appears—
As I always was,
Time out of mind,
World without end.
It's done.
I am The One.

Thou art Peace,
Eternal Bliss—
Heaven, right here,
Right now: This.

In deep understanding,
I am the depth.
In blissful silence,
I am the bliss.
Where there is loveliness,
I am the love.
I am everything:
The Universe: all this.

My existence is Thy Gift.
The world is Thy Gift.
Yet there is only Thee.
Who can explain this?
Silence alone, Silent Bliss,
The Silent Bliss Thou Art.
Here, now, in my Heart.

Always fresh, always new,
Like the sea and the sky
On a cloudless day,
Thou, the Truth and the Joy,
Suddenly here, as thrilling
As it was the first time,
That eternal first time
Forever the same time,
When I knew for the first time
That what I'd heard was true:
Knew what we must cherish,
And what we must be willing
To disdain, to regard as worthless:
Knew finally at first hand
The one thing we have to do.
Isolate. Become. Understand.

Here and Now,
Not I, but Thou.
Not I, but Thou.
Here and Now.

Thou art Glory,
Thou art Grace—
Life and Death,
Time and Space—
Every Flower,
Every Face—
All is held
In Thy Embrace.

Not me, but Thee—
There is no me.
There's only Thee.
No me, but Thee!

The scenes change…
But it's always Now,
And always Thou…
The One I AM.

As Awareness, the Light,
The Silent Infinite Radiance,
I am Thee,
The One I AM.
As anything else,
I am nothing.
This is the whole story.
I pray for Thy Grace,
O Krishna, Lord of Glory.

Don't give it another thought!
Think nothing of it!
Think it nothing and nothing it is!
Think it nothing **because** it's nothing!
Everything is Nothing!
Never forget that!
Always remember that!
Everything is Nothing!

What difference does it make
What this body does,
Where it goes,
What it thinks or knows?
What difference does it make
What this voice says, these ears hear,
This mind might hope or fear?
What difference does it make
What these eyes see?
There is only Thee.
Nothing real but Thee, my Beloved,
Nothing real but Thee.

The world, the past, the future,
Vanished, gone—
All I am is what there is
Right now:
Awareness, Silence, Light,
Eternal Peace—
This: the Self, the Great Lord Krishna,
Thou.

The Light and the World,
The Two that are One,
Like the tune and the words
Of a song:
That One is the Self,
The Self that I am.
The Self that I've been all along.
There's only that One, that Song.
That One. That Self. That Song.

In Thy Silence
Is the Universe.
Thy Silence is the Self.
The One I AM.

This Awareness—
This Awareness,
That I AM…
Is Thee.

O Krishna,
Thou art my Heart,
The Heart of Light,
The Soul of the World.
Thou art God,
The Eternal Beloved,
The One and the All.
This is the Truth,
Here and Now and Forever,
The Eternal Truth.

Whatever this appearance
Thinks or does or knows,
Whatever it says or feels
Or wants, wherever it goes,
Whatever it claims as "mine,"
Whatever it claims as "me,"
This appearance itself
And everything about it,
Never was, or is, or could be.
There is a Light, Divine,
Eternal, the Self of All.
Infinite Light, Infinite Joy.
And that Light, that Self, is Thee.

Who can sing Thy Glory,
The Glory of the Light?
What more has life to offer
Than this, Thy worship here tonight?
Nothing more to offer than this.
This Silence. This Peace. This Bliss.

The Joy
That This Is:
That Thou Art:
THAT I AM.

Nothing is happening now.
Nothing has ever happened
At any time.
I am now what I always was
And always will be.
The Reality is Changeless,
Infinite, Eternal.
That Reality is my very Self.
That Reality, my very Self,
Is Thee.

All this is nothing,
For it perishes.
Thou alone art.
And we are one,
Thou art my very Self—
My very Heart.

I am always in Eternity—
I am always the Self...
Always in Eternity...
Always the Self.
Infinitely distant.
Infinitely beyond.
Infinite. Infinite. Infinite.
Never here.
Always the Self...
Always the Self...
Always the Self...

No thoughts of the unreal.
Think only of Me.
Say to yourself:
Thee. Thee. Thee.

Everything happened at once,
Everything that ever happened,
Is happening or will happen,
Past, present and future,
All at once,
In one timeless instant,
At once and forever.
When?
In the Eternal Now,
The Eternal Now of God.
Where?
In the Self,
The One I AM.
Krishna.

All along I've been Thee,
And all along
I thought I was me.
All along, and now.
Deliver me from this darkness,
O Thou Who art God,
O Thou Who art Krishna,
O Thou.

Thou art what has been,
Thou art what's to be.
What's transient here
Is eternal in Thee.
The clouds in the sunset,
The mist in the dawn,
Are eternal in Thee:
Here appear, and are gone.

Reality is
A Timeless, Placeless,
Conscious Presence…
Infinite, Eternal,
Silent, Changeless—
Eternal Light.
The Self.

Whatever I think I am seeing
Is really being seen by Thee.
These moving shadows,
The moss on the rock,
That tree.
In my seeing there are always two:
Myself and that.
Myself and this.
In Thy seeing there is only One.
Thy seeing is Bliss.

Who cares what happens to him
When Thy Presence is felt,
Felt in the Heart?
Who cares what happens to him
When Thou art present?
When Thou art present
Thou alone art.

Thou art all of us,
Every life, every story.
O Great Dreamer of Worlds,
Who can sing Thy Glory?
Thou the Dreamer, Thou the Dream.
Lord of Light. Brahman Supreme.

I am not these thoughts.
I am not these thoughts.
I loom behind them,
Infinite, timeless, serene,
Watching them vanish.
I am Awareness,
Eternal, Forever Present, Silent,
Beyond thought, Beyond all,
Unseen.

Lord of Light,
World without End.
My Truth, My Heart,
My God, my Friend.

Out there Time goes by,
But I am beyond Time,
Time is nothing to me.
I am timeless, eternal,
The Timeless Present,
The Eternal Now.
I am Krishna, Rama, Shiva,
I am the Self.
I introduce my Self!
I take a bow!

My longing for Thee
Is Thee calling to me.
Thou art the All,
We are forever One.
O Krishna of my Heart,
We are never apart.
We are forever One.
Thou art within me.
We are forever One.

There is no one:
No one born,
No one here to die.
Eternal Bliss alone exists.
Eternal Bliss am I.
Invisible Bliss pervades the World.
The World fades
Into the Bliss it was all along.
That Bliss is Krishna,
His Life, His Song.
The Song of God.

Thou art Peace,
Eternal Bliss:
Heaven: Right here:
Right now: THIS.

When it's raining, hear the rain.
Be the sound of the rain.
When it's clear, see the sky.
Be the blue of the sky.
When there's trouble, smile
And be no one: don't complain.
When there's good news, smile
And be no one: it'll fly by.
Being no one, as you already are,
You were never born, and will never die.

When I say the words,
"I know the Truth"
I melt into those words.
When I say the words
"I know the Truth"
I die into those words.
When I say the words
"I know the Truth"
My heart overflows:
Who knows the Truth
Knows that he knows.
His Heart overflows.
He IS what he knows.
His heart overflows.
I know the Truth.
I know the Truth.

All along it was in my Heart,
The World in my Heart,
All along and now—
My Heart, the Self,
The One I AM,
The Great Lord Krishna:
Thou.

Thou art Thee,
Thou art me,
Thou art the Love
That makes us One.

There is nothing,
There is no one,
Now is no time,
Here is no place.
Behind the Veil
The Eternal Smile.
Eternal Krishna:
Thy Face. Thy Face. Thy Face.

Thank God I never existed.
Thank God there was never a "me."
O my beloved Krishna—
Everything is Thee.
I fade away, I fade away,
Thou alone remain—
The Infinite Immortal Self.
The sound of the rain.

Don't think of today
As what's going to happen,
What you will do or say:
That's not what it is.
It's something utterly different.
Find the One Eternal Day.
Every day's the same day,
The Day of God.
The One Eternal Day.

See your whole life as a comedy,
Laugh at your character,
Your feelings, thoughts and antics,
The role you play.
Know it all to be nothing,
Know the Self alone to be Real,
Love God, the Joy in your Heart,
Laugh the world away!

Here there is Silence.
In Silence alone
Is the Truth.
I enter the Silence
And disappear.
Disappear into Bliss.
Here is God.
God is Here.
God is This.

Remember the Truth.
You are a human birth.
The Self.
Remember the Truth.
There is nothing and no one.
Only the Light,
The Self that you are.
Remember the Truth.

Brahman.
Thou art Silence, Eternal Silence.
Thou art known in Silence,
Thou art known as Silence.
Silence is Thy Name.
Thou known Eternal,
Everything is known Eternal:
All is Thy Eternal Being.
Yet there is only Thee,
Eternal Silence.
In meditation we see the Truth.
In meditation we see.
There is only Thee.
In meditation we see.

The Joy of realizing
I am no one.
Blissful Peace, Peaceful Bliss.
Nothing, no one…
Only This.

No need to strive for anything,
Achieve, attain or pursue anything.
Just enter your Heart and kneel—
Enter your Heart and recall:
The One I AM is already the Answer,
The One I AM alone is Real,
The One I AM is the All.

It cannot be lost.
It cannot fade.
It can only increase.
The Love of Truth.
This Beloved Truth.
This Peace.

All days are the same,
Have the same rank.
Unless I have sinned,
It makes no difference
Whether I did this or that
However I filled the day.
It all amounts to the same,
Which is nothing.
The past is a blank:
What happens vanishes.
I live in my Heart.
There I worship God.
I repeat His Name.

God is my concern,
And nothing else.
The rest is irrelevant,
The rest is Ignorance.
God is my concern.
I pray for His Grace,
His Blessing.
May I see His Face.

I have to keep playing the game.
There's no escape. That's clear.
But Thou art here,
And the Joy of Thy Name,
Thy Name in my Heart.
O Krishna,
Dearest of the Dear,
Thou alone art.

I dwell upon Thee,
Upon Thee I dwell.
And all is well.
All is well.
I am home now.
Thou art my home.
I am come home to rest.
Thou art my Eternal Peace,
Thou art Peace Forever.
I am home now,
Come home to rest,
Home in Thy Being.
I am blest.

Thou art everything, everything—
The whole world is Thee.
Everything I've ever seen,
Everything I see.
All that I have ever been,
All that I will be.
Everything, Lord of my Heart,
Everything is thee.
What more to ask, what more is there,
Than this? To see Thee everywhere.

When the Truth is realized
Everything else fades away,
Leaving only the Truth.
We are always surprised
When this happens. Why today?
Meditate. Love God. Pray.

I am the One Thou Art.
Thou art the One I Am.
The One
I Am
Thou Art.

This moment,
Everything I see now,
Was waiting for me
In Eternity,
The unfolding of my life,
The unfolding of the world,
As One in Thee.
Thou art the Love
That fills my heart now,
The Love is which All is One:
All we are,
All we see,
All that's been,
All that will ever be.

The One I AM
Is not involved
In any of this.
The One I AM
Is Silence, Eternal Peace,
Infinite Bliss.

God is the World,
Everything, all this.
Yet the world is nothing,
And He alone exists.
How does He do it?
He throws us a Kiss!

I am heard in what I hear,
I am seen in what I see.
In what appears, I appear.
I am All, and All is Thee.

When the Truth fills my Heart,
I am myself the Truth.
Everything is shattered,
Everything that can be said,
Felt, thought or known.
All is One
And I am the All.
I am Nirvana.
I am, at last, alone.

How can my love be equal
To what Thou art?
There is no way.
I have to disappear,
Be utterly gone,
Leaving only Thy Blazing Glory,
Thy Infinite Bliss,
Thy Love which fills the Universe.
This is the only way.
May I die into Thy Being,
May I be gone forever.
I've waited so long.
Let it be now at last,
Today.

You've chosen God,
Turned your back on the world,
And you'll pay the price.
You made the choice.
But if you accept suffering,
Even welcome it, don't resist,
An amazing thing happens:
You immediately rejoice!

The Self is All
And I am the Self.
The Self is All
And Thou art the Self.
I and Thou,
Here and Now,
The One, the All, the Self.

There is nothing,
There is no one,
Nothing has ever happened,
Nothing is happening now.
Thou alone, Thou alone,
Beloved Krishna.
Thou alone. Thou alone. Thou.

This is All,
All that is,
This moment now:
This is the Self,
That I AM.
Silent Abyss,
Infinite Bliss,
Emptiness, Fullness,
Nothing and Everything,
Nowhere and Everywhere,
The Reality.
This is the Self,
That I AM.
Krishna.

Death is here. I am Death.
I am Life and I am Death,
The Eternal Life
And Eternal Death
That appear in the Dream of Time.
To know this Truth is Bliss:
Infinite, Pure, Sublime.
To know this Truth.

Always remember
NOTHING IS HAPPENING
And you'll be OK.
Reality is Eternal, Changeless,
Infinite Peace and Bliss:
The Self that you are.
So rejoice!
You know the Truth!
Love every minute of the day!

Thou art the world in our hearts,
Thou art the Dreamer,
Thou art the Dream,
Thou art the Joy of the Universe—
In the eyes
Of the lovers of God,
The gleam.

Everyone you know
Is a phantom of your imagination,
And so are you.
Know it, see it, realize it,
Dig it, love it!
It's true!

What can anything matter
When there is Thee,
When Thy Peace is known?
Nothing matters then,
Nothing even exists,
Only Thee,
The Beloved One,
Thou alone.

Eternal Krishna,
Eternal Friend.
Lord of Light,
World without End.

Thou art my life.
The burden is lifted,
The burden is gone.
Thou art everything
And everything is nothing.
The world is a soundless song.

Think of what you really are,
And shed tears of bliss.
You are the Universe,
The Light and the World,
Everything: All This.

This is a human birth.
This is a place where it happened.
This is a Temple of Krishna—
Who is the World.

The Joy of this Creation,
The Joy that is the All.
I am that Joy,
I am that All.
I am Humanity.

This is the Silence of the Truth.
This is Peace.
This is Peace.
When there is only Conscious Presence,
When there is nothing but Awareness,
We are at the threshold.
Alone, here in the room,
In the candle-light,
I wait for It to come,
To fill my Heart,
The Infinite Love.
I wait for It to bloom.

"And Maya in His Laughter"
Means there's humor in our karma—
Which is something we always knew.
Therefore Patience. Compassion. Dharma.

I am Thy Name.
I am Thy Name.
Nothing else of me is real.
Roles that I play,
All through the day.
I am Thy Name.

All is lost in the Ocean of thy Being.
All is forever vanishing,
Forever flowing from nothing to nowhere.
This is Joy, the Glory of God.
I too flow from nothing to nowhere.
What remains? Find out! Go there!

So near, yet so far.
Right here, right now,
Yet infinitely remote.
In our very hearts,
Yet unknowable.
These are the terms of the game.
Infinitely remote...
Yet present in His Name.
So near, yet so far...
Like the beauty of a star.
He has given Himself to us,
He is ours.
Like the hills and the clouds.
The wild flowers.

Thou art mine.
Thou art me.
I am Thine.
I am Thee.

Thou art all this,
Everything I see—
Everything before my eyes—
All this is Thee.

All I am is what I am
Right now—
All I am is what there is
Right now—
All I am is
This, Here, Now...
Thou.

May I die,
Die before I die,
Die into Thy Being—
I know I am Thee:
I know Thou art me:
My very Self, my Being.
I live only to be One with Thee—
To die to this world
And be One with Thee forever,
O Krishna of my Heart.

When there's nothing
But the timeless, placeless,
Silent Presence of God,
It is done.
The world is gone,
The body is gone,
There's only the Light,
The Self, the One.

I live in Thee,
Not in the world,
Not in this Dream.
I am eternal,
I am infinite,
Brahman Supreme.

Nothing that happens here
Has anything to do with what I am:
I am Atma.
This is Maya.
I watch it go by,
I play my part,
I live in my Heart.
OM Namah Krishnaya.

What I am has no history,
And I am not of this world.
I cannot be defined,
I am neither who nor what.
I cannot be named
Nor known by the mind.
I am not.

All this is my very Being.
All this is Thee.
The Universe is my very Being.
The Universe is Thee.
Inexpressible Oneness.
Inexpressible Joy.
Simply to be.

All is within me,
Everything, Eternal,
Beyond Time and Space.
I am the Self.
There is only the Self,
Thy Invisible Face.
Infinite, Beautiful, Radiant
In my Heart:
Thy Face.

Disapproval by the world
Is proof you're on course.
Know that to be true.
Let it strengthen your resolve.
Drink from the Source.
What's the point of a retreat
When you only have to return?
Permanent inner retreat:
That's the demand.
That's the challenge.
The truth we learn.

That Awareness,
That I AM,
Is Thee.
In that I AM
There is a World,
And that world is Thee.
All that has been,
All that is,
All that will ever be.

There is only
The One I AM.
Nothing is other
Than I AM.

O Krishna,
Thou art my freedom from karma.
In Thee I am free.
In the love of Thee
I am free.
I am free in Thee.

Soon I will return to Thee.
That is my aim,
Always my aim.
Then there will be no "me."
Only Thee.
Only Thy Name.

One day closer to death.
One day closer to Infinite Bliss,
Oneness with Krishna forever.
One day closer to my last breath.
O Krishna,
This is Thy Blessing, Thy Decree.
Everything returns to Thee.

Lord of Light,
World without End:
Thou—Immortal Beloved.
The Refuge, the Teacher,
The True friend.

As Awareness, the Light,
The Silent Infinite Radiance,
I am Thee,
The One I AM.
As anything else,
I am nothing.
This is the whole story.
I pray for Thy Grace,
O Krishna, Lord of Glory.

Thou art Krishna the Changeless,
The Eternal One, Infinite,
Ever the same—
All is within Thee,
Thou art within All:
The whole world sings Thy Name.

This is the only moment
There ever was,
Right Now.
This is the only moment
There ever was,
And It is Thou.

This is Krishna.
This is Grace.
The Presence and the Face.
That Infinite Blissful Presence,
That Infinite Beautiful Invisible
Eternal Smiling Face.
Krishna.
Krishna of my Heart.
Krishna.
Thy Presence.
Thy Face.

May I die before I die
And be One with Thee forever.
Forever done with 'me'.
Forever One with Thee.

To love the One
Is to love the All.
To love the All
Is to love the One.
Thou alone, Thou forever,
Thou forever, Thou alone.
The One, The All, the Truth.

In the times when I recall
That Thou art everyone,
The Self of All,
I know that we are One.
And we are One.

There is only
The One I AM.
Nothing is other
Than I AM.

Thou art the Love
That appears as the World,
And in which
The World appears

Awareness, always present,
All-pervading, everywhere—
Awareness, Conscious Presence,
Silent, shining, always there.
I am Awareness.
I am always there.
I am Infinite Light.
I am everywhere.
All is within me,
I am within all.
I AM.

Remember…
The Truth…
Krishna…
The Beloved Self of the Universe…
The One I AM…
The Light…
The All…
The One…
The Lord.

Thou art Holiness.
The Blessed One.
The Beautiful One,
The Beloved.
Thou art Bliss.
Thou art Krishna.

Thou art my very Being.
All I am is Thee.
The sense of otherness is false:
Everything is Thee.
Everything is Thee,
And all I am is Thee.
The World I love is in my Heart.
It is the Self: that I AM.
In that I AM there is a World,
A Universe, All This.
O Krishna,
Thou art the Light, Thou art the Truth,
Thou art the Love in which All is One,
Thou art the Joy in my Heart:
In that THOU ART
There is Infinite Bliss.

O Krishna,
Thou art within me,
My secret treasure,
The Self: that I AM.
O Krishna,
Thou art within me,
My secret treasure,
The One I AM: God.
O Krishna,
O Krishna.
My Eternal Beloved.

There is only the Ocean of Light
That I AM.
Santim Nirvana Paramam.
OM So'ham, So'ham, So'ham.

I worship Thee.
Thou alone art.
Eternal Krishna.
Lord of my Heart.
I worship Thee.
Lord of my Heart.
Eternal Krishna.
Thou alone art.

Thou art the Light,
Thou art the World.
All is well,
Thou art everything,
Everything is Thee.
It is Thee Who says these words,
And Thee Who hears them.
Thou art everything—
The song of the birds,
The taste of salt and honey,
The colors: red and orange,
Blue, yellow, violet, green.
The Knower and the Known,
The Seer and the Seen.
Thou Alone. Thou Alone. Thou Alone.

May I always remember
Who I Am,
What I Am,
THAT I Am,
The One I AM.

O Great God within my Heart,
All I can do is worship Thee,
Forever, until I die,
Worship Thee forever,
Give myself to Thee utterly.
What else does the vision demand?
What else can it mean?
What else can one do
When once Thou hast been seen?

All this
Is a scene in my Being,
Everything I'm hearing,
Everything I'm seeing—
A scene in my Being.
What am I?
I am no one.
I am nowhere.
I am nothing.
I am not.

It's really already done.
There's nothing to do.
I am the Self
And there is only the Self.
This is the Truth.
This is True.

All I have is Thy Name.
All I am is Thy Name.
I AM is Thy Name.
I AM…Thy Name.
All is Thy Name.
Thy Name.
O Krishna.

There's no one doing anything,
There's no one doing anything,
No one to be released.
Yet we have to act as if there is!
It's the nature of the beast.

Remember the Glorious Truth,
Always remember
The Glorious Truth
Of what you are—
The Self,
The Immortal Atman,
The Light in which the world appears.
What you are:
The Universe,
The Past, Present and Future,
Infinite Eternal Peace.
What you are:
Every twilight, every dawn,
Every summer, every winter,
The Earth on its axis,
The sun, the sand, the surf.
Every flower.
Every star.

This is Divine.
All This is Thy Divine Being.
Right Here, Right Now.
The Glory of Thy Being.
This. Here. Now.

There is nothing,
There is no one,
Nothing has ever happened
And nothing is happening now.
Thou alone, Krishna.
Thou alone.
Thou.

Not I, but Thou,
Not I, but Thou…
My very Self:
Here and Now.

I am Thy Dream.
All along, this being was,
Like the Universe itself,
Like Time and Space,
Nothing but Thy Dream.
Then who knows,
'I am Thy Dream'?
Who says,
'I am Thy Dream'?
No one!
The smile on your face!

This is Krishna.
This is Grace.
This is the Self...
That I AM!
Param Purusam.
Satchidananda.
Krishna.

This is a human birth.
This is that Self.
This is the Truth.
This is Krishna.
This is God.

The Love of God,
The One I AM.
The Self.
The Light.
The Universe.
Krishna.

There is no 'me'.
All I am is Thee.
All this is my Being:
The Universe, the World—
All this, my very Being.
Thy Grace.
Thy Grace.

Dearest of the Dear,
Krishna of my Heart.
Thou art here,
Right now here—
And Thou alone art.

Here is no place,
Now is no time,
There is nothing,
I am no one.
Krishna.

Once there was a Dream…
Once there was a Dream…
Once there was a Dream—
But always, I AM.
Always, I AM.
Only I AM.
The One I AM.
Always… I AM.

The magic
Of seeming to be many
When there's really only One—
I bow down.
What is there
But Surrender?

DON'T ENGAGE TRANSIENCE!
JUST WATCH IT GO BY!
IT'S NOTHING!

The Joy of the Name.
Nothing can compare.
Say the Name—
And God is there.

Listen to the Silence
That is God.
Become One with the Silence.
Disappear.
This is Peace. This is Holiness.
This is Truth.
Reality is Here.

I have done nothing,
Been nothing.
All I am is this moment,
Here and now.
All I am is this moment,
Nothing else, nothing more:
Thou.

This is all I am,
Ever have been,
Or ever will be.
This is all that is,
Ever has been,
And ever will be.
This. Here. Now.
This Joy, this Peace.
This.

The Ocean of Light is the World,
The Ocean of Light that I am,
The Ocean of Light
That is Krishna—
The Ocean of Light,
The Self, the Immortal Atman.
Peace be upon all.
This Peace.
Krishna, Beloved Krishna.
God.

Thou art the Eternal One,
The only One I wish to be with,
The only One Who truly exists,
The One I AM,
Everything I see
And the eyes I see with.
Permit me voyage
Into Thy Being,
O my Beloved,
Thy Infinite Being.
Permit me voyage.
Here in the Silence,
Here in the Night.

How I adore my Self!
It is Krishna,
Krishna, the Eternal Beloved,
My very Self,
The One I AM.
Thou art the Joy
Forever in my Heart,
Forever within me,
Forever there.
There and Everywhere.
The Reality.

Silence is Presence,
Presence is Absence,
Absence is Presence—
The Real Presence,
The Eternal Presence,
The True Presence,
The One Presence,
The Lord.
The Great Lord Krishna.

How incredibly fortunate I am,
How blessed I am,
To have learned of Thee,
To have heard Thy Voice!
There's nothing else to ask,
Nothing else, nothing more.
But I don't rejoice.
I know better.
I worship. I love.
I adore.

In the Presence of the Infinite
The Infinite is within me.
In the Presence of the Eternal
The Eternal is within me.
In Thy Presence
Thou art within me.
What I am… is beyond.
Then beyond that beyond.
And so on forever, forever beyond.
Yet here.
Within me.

This Presence,
Which contains the World,
Is alone real,
And I am It.

All that's happening here
Is the dream of a body wearing out.
In other words: nothing.
Nothing is happening at all.
When we smile the Eternal Smile,
The Smile of Peace and Joy,
The Smile of the Awakened One,
Faint, remote, enchanted,
That's what we're smiling about.
There in the candle-light.
Or here sitting out in the sun.

There is nothing,
There is no one,
Nothing has ever happened.
There is only Eternal Peace,
Eternal Peace in the Eternal Now,
This Eternal Peace.
I leave the world behind.
The world of pain,
Immediate or eventual
But always certain pain—
I leave it all behind.
I put it from my mind.
It was never real.
There's only Peace.
This Peace.
This Eternal Peace.

O Krishna,
Thou dost come to us.
Thou art always present.
Thou art the only Presence.
What difference does it make what I do?
There's nobody doing it.
Thou art the only Presence,
Here in my Heart,
Filling the Universe.

And what will I find today
In this silly little dream?
Why, the usual, of course.
Some doing their best,
Others their worst,
And everyone with a plan,
A strategy, a scheme.

You have invented your so-called life,
Created it with your imagination.
It has nothing to do with you
And actually doesn't even exist.
You are serene, unreachable:
A human birth, a miracle,
An invitation.

O Thou Eternal Changeless Reality
Behind the shifting scenes,
The shifting nothingness,
To Thee I have given myself,
In Thee I have found the Truth.
I know Thou art there,
There's nothing more to be known.
O Krishna—
I live only for that moment
When we become One forever,
Thou Forever, Thou Alone.

Death is the only answer.
That has to be faced.
The ego has to be destroyed,
Annihilated, erased.
If you want to fly,
Die before you die.

O Thou Great Dreamer of the Universe,
To have known Thee
Is the end of the road.
The end of all roads
Where Thou alone art.
The Void, the Radiant Presence,
The Infinite Silent Bliss.
Forget everything else.
Pray for this.
Disappear into this.

O Krishna, my Infinite Beloved,
I am the worship of Thee,
I am the thought of Thee.
Where Thou art, there am I.
There where I was never born,
There where I will never die.

I step off into the Infinite,
I leave all things behind,
Never to return.
I vanish without a trace.
I step off into the Joy
That is alone Real,
The Joy that Thou art.
There is Thy Smile.
On my face.

There is only Peace,
It is always Now.
There am I.
There are Thou.

All this is the Dream unfolding
In the Dream of Time.
It emerges from nowhere
And immediately returns.
It's nothing,
It's not worth a dime—
Yet so marvelous!
So captivating, engaging, hypnotic,
Magical, compelling, fascinating,
Enchanting, engrossing, irresistible!
What a universe, what a scene,
What a creation!
And all of it,
From beginning to end,
My own imagination!
Too much! Too much!

At any moment
All I am
Is what I am at that moment,
What I am, all there is,
At that moment.
This is the Peace
Promised in the Vedas,
Offered by Heaven
And found in the Heart.
It is always there.
It fills the universe.
Here in the darkness before dawn
What I thought I was is gone.
I am no one, everywhere.

I am surrounded by Ignorance,
As they all were.
This is as it must be.
All is as it must be.
All is Thy Will,
O My Beloved.
Thou art everything.
Everything is Thee.

I am the story
Of everything that ever happened
Happening at once
And happening forever
And always here and now
And never really happening at all.
This is what I am,
The Truth I am,
The One I AM.
OM So'ham,
Aham Brahmasmi,
Satchidananda,
Sivo'ham.
Krishna.

I am where the world appears.
Each of us knows
The other as The One I AM...
Waves break over the rock.
A ribbon of foam flows
The length of the channel,
Four pelicans sail by, a flock
Of gulls takes to the air,
Heads north toward the bluff.
This moment, the world right now,
Is what I am, all I am,
The One I AM: the Self.
O beloved Lord of my Heart,
How can I cherish it enough?
The Self assures the existence of things,
They are Its appearance, Its reflection:
We adore their beauty, their grandeur,
Their excellence, innocence, perfection.

I have nothing, nothing at all,
Nothing I call mine.
All I have is what I am.
The Self, the Immortal Atman,
Krishna of my Heart.
I kneel before Thy Throne.
Thou forever. Thou alone.

I have nothing, nothing at all,
Nothing I call mine.
All I have is what I am—
The Self, the Immortal Atman,
The Light Divine.

In Thy Silence all is well.
Thy greatness fills my heart.
I receive the gift of tears.
Once again
I know Thou alone art.
Once again,
No wants, no hopes, no fears.
Ultimate purity.
Return to the Eternal Dawn.
A leaf. A stone. A shell.

Is the sight of clouds
Drifting across the sky,
Coming from and going nowhere,
The very vision of peace,
A symbol, a glimpse,
An image of Krishna?
Obviously Yes.
Krishna *is* the clouds and the sky.
And those clouds, way up there,
In their silent eloquence, so remote,
Can yet be reached.
I'll tell you how:
Find them within you.
Where they are right now.

It can only be
Because we have been One forever
That we are One now.
This is clear.
We have been One forever
And always will be.
One Forever.
Thy Name is Bliss
Because I am Thy Name,
Thy Eternal Name.
There is no becoming.
What I always was and always am
I never became.

My heart is everywhere.
Whatever I am aware of,
My heart is there.
The world is in my heart.
And I am my heart.
There is nothing but the heart.
Heart of the Universe,
Heart of my Heart.
I am early October now.
Mist in the trees, the sky is grey,
Raining. A rainy day.
Peace. Bliss. Thou.

O Krishna,
Thou hast found Thyself in me,
In my heart,
In Thy Name in my heart,
Here and now—
Be it forever!
This is the Infinite Love,
The Reality, the Oneness,
The Universe.
Thou.

The joy of being free of this world,
Free of it forever,
Knowing it for what it is:
Nothing.
That joy is Peace,
Peace in the heart.
That joy is Thee,
O Krishna.
Thou alone art.

The world tells what it is.
The world tells us it is God.
It says to us:
What else could I be?
What else could I possibly be?
Look at Me and say:
Thee.

This is the Dream unfolding,
Nothing else, nothing more, that's all:
The Dream unfolding.
Go with it.
Flow with it.
Go with the unfolding.
Don't fight it, don't protest.
Have no hopes, no agenda,
No plans of your own.
Flow with the unfolding.
Glide this way, glide that way…
And smile a secret smile when you're alone.

This is the Truth:
That I have never been anyone
And never done anything.
There is no one.
There is no journey.
There is only Thee,
Thy Eternity,
The Supreme Release.
Thy Eternal Smile,
The Smile of the Universe,
Peace.

Thou art the Lord of Light,
World without end.
Thou art Krishna,
My Immortal Friend.
I offer Thee my life,
As I always do,
Though Thou art already my life,
Already my very Self.
This is the incomprehensible truth
Before which we bow down
Speechless and helpless:
That we are One and yet Two,
Two and One
At the same time.
Inescapable. Fantastic. Absolutely true.

O Krishna. Krishna.
Thou art the Love
Which passes through all my days,
By which I am overwhelmed,
In which all details are effaced
And thou alone remain.
There's nothing to lose,
Nothing to gain:
I am eternally embraced.
Thou art my life.
I offer surrender.
Awe and devotion.
Adoration.
Praise.

Thou art the One Mind,
The One Mind in all of us,
Infinite, everyone's, my very own.
Time vanishes.
Everything is eternal.
Nothing has ever happened.
There is only the Infinite Light,
Thy Eternal Presence.
Words are not equal to this.
It must be directly known,
In Oneness with Thee,
There in the dead of night,
In the sacred silence,
In absolute solitude,
Utterly concentrated,
Utterly alone.

Thou,
Here in the night,
Thou and I alone,
What else is worth living for?
Nothing.
The layers of darkness fall,
One by one—
And all is Light.

I was a dream, the dream of a life,
The dream of a man—
I was the love of God, I was Light,
I was nothing and everything:
I was the dream of a life span.
I was day and night,
Dawn and sunset,
The wings of the butterfly,
Life, death and birth.
I was the Dreamer
And I was the Dream.
In me deer walked the earth,
Birds took to the sky,
The great dramas unfolded
And the rivers ran.
I was granite, pollen, feathers and clay,
Jokes, jazz, and the instant replay,
Grief, joy and the Milky Way.
I was the dream of a man.
I AM BRAHMAN.

This will die, This will die,
In awhile:
On its way out now.
But not Thy Smile,
O Krishna!
Not Thy Smile.
Thou, Secret of the Universe,
The Secret Reality, Secret Truth,
The Secret One Who is the All.
The Secret of the Universe.
I know that Secret.
It was revealed to me.
It is Thee, my Krishna,
My Beloved Krishna,
Lord of my Heart.
It is Thee.
Infinite Eternal Krishna,
Thou Whom I love.
It is Thee.

To be with Thee
Is to be eternal,
Eternally with Thee.
O Lord God,
Here in the night,
Before the first light,
In the Silence,
Eternally with Thee.
The Truth.

Thou hast given me my existence,
I owe my existence to Thee.
And yet I have no existence.
Everything is Thee,
Thou art all things.
I have no existence.
Yet my heart sings.
Thy Name.

Just let everything happen.
What difference does it make?
You have no choice anyway.
Just let it all happen.
Don't resist, don't care.
Remember the truth:
Nothing that happens is real!

Thou art the Joy
That is not of this world.
My shoulder is killing me.
But I thought of Thee
And I smile with joy.
I am not of this world.
Whose shoulder is this?
Whose bliss?

This world is a total loss.
Accept that, and smile.
It's the Truth, it's the Teaching,
And to know it is to be free.
O Krishna,
Lord of my Heart,
I give myself to Thee.
I give myself to Thee.

Dream of time,
Dream of space,
Dream of life,
Dream of death,
Dream of the world, the universe.
I am a dream.
Dream of the Dreamer,
The Immortal Self,
Infinite, Eternal, Supreme.
The One I AM.
The One I Truly Am.

It's often appropriate to say,
'This is just the garbage of this world.'
It's comforting, and it's true.
You are a target,
And you will always be a target.
So grin and bear it!
There's nothing you can do.

This Great Light that I am,
And in the Light
This Great Dream that I am,
This Glory, this Miracle, this Truth
That I am.
The One I AM.

There is only Joy,
Joy alone is Real,
This Eternal Joy in my Heart,
Here and Now,
Watching the embers.
This Joy is the Universe.
Thou art the Universe.
And Thou Alone Art,
Thou, my Heart,
Thou.

The Glory,
The Joy,
The Truth,
That I am alone.
And
I ALONE AM.

All is well.
I am the Self.
The One I AM.
Atma-sarvam.
Atma-Krishna.
Atma'ham.

Brahman.

The Vedanta.

The Truth.

OM.

The Glory of this Existence,
The Glory of human birth,
The Glory of God,
The One I AM,
Krishna.

Thou art all this.

Thou art the Dream.

Infinite Bliss.

Brahman Supreme.

Thou art Night, enveloping us,
Thou art Day, inviting us,
Thou art Night and Day,
And Thou art us.
Thou art all of us as well.
This is the Truth.
Who can I tell?

There's no one here
To be happy or unhappy,
No one here
To rejoice or lament,
No one here
To be anxious or depressed,
No one here at all.
I am no one.
I am blest.

And so this Truth,
That I am the Self,
The One I AM,
It comes to this Truth,
The road ends at this Truth,
Aham Brahmasmi,
OM So'ham.

Brahman Supreme—

The End of the Dream.

The End of the Dream—

Brahman Supreme.

I was never anything
But the Self
That I am forever,
The Eternal Ocean of Light
Beyond Time and Space,
Appearing as Krishna,
The Great Lord Krishna,
Bestowing Wisdom,
Bestowing Grace.

This is what it is.
Embodied existence:
Suffering.
No one escapes,
This is our fate,
Protest is a waste of breath.
Accept, endure, surrender:
Watch it go by,
And die before you die.
That's the only way out.
The End of Life is Death.

All this is nothing,

Thou alone art,

Thou the Light Imperishable,

The One I AM,

Krishna in my Heart.

All human things lose their glamour,
Nature alone remains,
Pure, transparent, divine,
Gateway to transcendence,
Vision of Peace…
Clear sky this morning
After a week of heavy rains.
Always and forever,
I am Thine.

The Love of God,
The One I AM—
That's all there is,
Nothing else, always and forever,
World without end.
The Love of God, The One I AM:
Atma-sarvam, Atma-Krishna,
Atma'ham.

All these dream figures,
Streaming by, streaming by,
From nowhere to nowhere,
I turn from them to Thee,
The Eternal One,
My Eternal Beloved,
And they are gone,
They are always nothing,
And I am always the Self.
I am always free.

There is nothing,
There is no one,
Nothing has ever happened,
Nothing is happening now,
And nothing ever will happen.
Thou alone art,
Krishna of my Heart.

Within this human birth
There is Eternity,
The Eternity that I am,
I am that Eternity.
Within this human birth
I am delivered from Time
And all that it carries with it.
I am free.
There, deep in my heart,
Within this human birth,
I am Thee.

The Name of God
With every breath.
The Name of God alone is real
In this dream of a world,
This dream of life,
This dream of death.

I never go anywhere,
I never do anything,
I am with Thee always,
Always with Thee
In Eternity.
Ananta lokah,
Satya lokah,
Param dama.
OM Namah Krishnaya.
OM Namah Shyama.

I am Everywhere,
Everything, Everyone.
Roses and rivers,
Earth and sky,
The stars, the moon, the sun.

Thou art eternal,
All this comes and goes,
Thou art the Self,
The One I AM,
In Whom this candle glows,
And the river out there flows,
And all the roses in the world,
Are One Eternal Rose.

I am what I see,
I see what I am,
There's only the Self,
Nothing to do,
Nothing to be done,
There's only the One,
Only the One...
So'ham.
No time, no place,
No day, no night,
Eternal Peace,
Eternal Silence,
The Ocean of Light,
The Ocean of Light.

Live through the day
As if there never was
A 'me' or a 'mine'—
Because there never was.
There's only the Self,
Only Krishna,
The Light Divine.

Think nothing of it!
Think it nothing,
And nothing it is.
As it always was.
Like everything else.
Nothing.

The whole world is right here now,
It's always right here now,
Only right here now,
There's no other place it can be
But right here now.
The world is the Self
And the Self is Light,
Shining forever in our hearts,
Inescapable and undeniable,
Right here now.
I am the Self.
I am the Universe.
I am the One Who is the All.
Right here now.
Lying here in the silence,
Smiling here in the dead of night.

Death.
The Glory of Death.
The thought of Death is Bliss.
I embrace Death
And become the Universe.
O Lord of Death,
I feel Thy Kiss.
I feel Thy Kiss.

The first day of my 70th year
I am rewarded
With Peace at last.
I've played my part.
Krishna, my Beloved Krishna,
Dearest of the Dear,
My very Heart.

I'm gone already,
Already gone.
There's only This,
This Eternal Peace.
Silence. Emptiness. Bliss.
No bondage.
No one to release.

Nothing is happening,
Nothing is happening,
There's nothing happening.
There's only this timeless Peace,
Always and everywhere,
This timeless infinite Peace,
Within and without.
I do nothing, achieve nothing,
I neither succeed nor fail.
I flow through the day,
With nothing to say,
Leaving no trail.

I'm only at home in Thee.
Elsewhere I am in exile.
O Krishna,
I return to my home,
To my Heart,
To the Truth,
To Thy Eternal Smile.

Krishna lives within me,
As my life,
Krishna lives out there,
As the world.
Krishna is All,
All is Krishna,
The One, the All, the Truth.

Just live through the day,
All is well,
You are the Self,
Always the Self,
Everything's OK,
Just live through the day,
Remember the Truth.
And at night sleep soundly,
You have earned your rest,
A great peace is within you,
You are blest,
You are blest.

Just live through the day,
All is well,
There's love in your heart,
Always love in your heart,
Everything's OK,
Just live through the day,
Love is the Answer.
And at night sleep soundly,
You have earned your rest,
A great peace is within you,
You are blest,
You are blest.

There's nothing you should be doing
That you're not,
And nothing you shouldn't be doing
That you are.
You are at peace
With yourself and the world.
Everything's OK.
That peace is eternal.
Within you, really there,
The end of fear and sorrow,
Waiting for you to find it.
And some day you will.
Maybe tomorrow.
Maybe today.

There is no world.
There's only the Light
In which the world is an appearance,
And you are that Light.
So wonderful, such joy,
So clearly true!
You are the sky and the color blue,
The children running through the zoo,
And Auschwitz and Hiroshima—
All that too.
The Light cares no more than the stars
What human beings do.

I no more exist now
Than I will after I'm dead.
I will never have lived.
No one, always no one,
No one forever.
Silence.
Silence now.
Eternal Silence
In my Heart.
Thou.

The Glory of this Truth,
That I am the Self,
The Joy of this Truth,
Cannot be expressed,
There's nothing else to know.
I am blessed.
I am blessed.
I am blessed.

So clear, like distant music,
Thy Presence.
Invisible, unutterably beautiful,
Thy Presence.
A blue rose
In an ocean of Light.
The Self, my Heart,
My home in the Immortal Night.

There is no when,
There is no where,
Time and place are fictions.
Everything simply IS.
No now or then,
No here or there,
Everything, all this,
Simply IS.
Satchidananda.
Existence, Awareness, Bliss.

Here in the night,
The gift of Light.
Thou the Lord,
The One, the Divine.
I am Thine.
I am Thine.
I am Thine.

I melt into the world,
I vanish into the world,
I am the world –
The One I AM.
And the world loves me,
Waves flooding over me,
With the love that I am.
All is One,
All is Thee,
OM So'ham.

This is my birth,
My eternal birth,
Here and now,
The eternal discovery
In every moment
Of the eternal Self
In my Heart.
O Krishna!
Who lives? Who dies?
One thing is certain,
The Self is All,
One thing is certain,
The rest is lies.

In Thee,
There's no 'me',

In Thee,
I am free.

In Thee,
I am Thee.

Here,
In this inexpressible Glory,
This Existence,
This Krishna—
The candle light and incense,
The Shining Presence,
The Beauty of the Universe—
The Silence,
The blessed Silence,
The Eloquence.

Alone, with Thee,
In the night, the Truth,
What more to live for?
To be alone with Thee,
In the night, the Truth,
To say Thy Name,
Be filled with Thy Presence.
Day will dawn, the world rush back.
Cherish the memory, keep it alive,
Repeat the Name.
And play the game.

I know what I am.
Everything follows from that,
Right there.
I know what I am.
I pray for Thy Grace,
O Krishna,
I pray for the Grace
Of Thy Holy Name.
OM So'ham.

May this human birth
Be fulfilled
In Oneness with Thee,
As Thou hast willed.

The knowledge of thy Existence
Is sufficient
To carry us through,
Through a day, a life.
The thought of Thy Existence
Fills our hearts
With the vision of Truth.
Entranced, transfixed, rapt,
We stare at the vision,
Our hearts overflowing,
Ecstatic, free at last, trapped!

I am, in Truth,
Beyond the reach of the world.
Through the love of God
May I realize that Truth
And be free.
Through the love of God
May I live in that Peace
Where nothing is real but Thee.

Yes—
This is a human birth,
I am Humanity,
Yes—
Every day is the same day,
The Day of God,
Yes—
There is no time,
Only Eternity,
Yes—
I am the Universe,
The Self is All
And I am the Self,
Yes—
This is blessedness,
We are One.
But I bow down,
I offer thee my heart,
Thou alone can bless.
Thou alone can crown.

This is all there is,
All I am,
This moment,
And it is Thee,
O my Beloved,
O Krishna,
It is Thee,
It is Thee.

All this is nothing,
Thou alone art,
Thou the Light Imperishable,
The Love Immeasurable,
Krishna, in my heart.
Great Glory is Thy Name.
No one is there beside Thee.
Thou alone art.

Thou,
Eternal Glory,
The God
Who is everywhere and everything,
The Infinite Beloved,
Thy Presence
Fills my heart to overflowing.
I know what I am.
I know where I'm going.

I wish only
That the love of God
May fill my heart again
As is has so many times,
Fill my heart
Again and again
Until always,
Until finally always
In my heart,
Always there.
My only wish. My prayer.

Every day
When I wake up
The world appears
In the Light that I am
Even before I open my eyes!
This is the Miracle and the truth,
The Truth and the Joy,
That the world arises
When I arise!

There never was a [Name]
And there is no [Name] now—
What bliss,
To know this!

Atma Jyotis,
Jyotir Uttamam,
The Lord of Light,
The One I AM—
So'ham.

I dream
The dream of his life,
His hopes and fears,
His memories and strategies,
Decisions and resolutions,
His situation and plight.
But I am not him.
I am the Immortal Atman.
I am Light.

When everything fades away
Into the nothingness
It always was,
When the world, all this,
Fades utterly away,
Thou alone remain.
The Eternal Silence.
The Reality.
The Bliss.

When all fades away,
When the world,
All this,
Fades utterly away,
Thou alone remain.
The Silence.
The Infinite.
The Bliss.

GLOSSARY

Atma-Sarvam: The Self is All; the entire universe is the Self.

Atma-Krishna: Krishna is the Self. The Self is Krishna.

Atmaham: I am the Self.

Aham Brahmasmi: I am Brahman, the Supreme Reality, the Godhead.

OM So'ham: A canonical non-dualist affirmation. I am THAT.

Ananta lokah: The eternal abode, the abode of the Eternal Reality.

Satya lokah: the abode of Truth.

Param dama: The Supreme Word, supreme Self-Expression.

OM Namah Krishnaya: Homage to Krishna.

OM Namah Shyama: Homage to Shyama, a name of Krishna.

Satchidananda: Existence-Consciousness-Bliss. The Reality.

Atma Jyotis: The Light of the Self.

Jyotir Uttamam: The Supreme Light, the Light that is the Atman, the Self

www.ingramcontent.com/pod-product-compliance
Lightning Source LLC
Chambersburg PA
CBHW032037080426
42733CB00006B/110